TOP 10 BASEBALL MANAGERS

David Pietrusza

SPORTS TOP 10

Enslow Publishers, Inc.

44 Fadem Road   PO Box 38
Box 699   Aldershot
Springfield, NJ 07081   Hants GU12 6BP
USA   UK

Library of Congress Cataloging-in-Publication Data

Pietrusza, David, 1949–
    Top 10 baseball mangers / David Pietrusza.
        p. cm. — (Sports top 10)
    Includes bibliographical references (p. 46) and index.
    Summary: Profiles ten successful managers in professional baseball: Felipe
Alou, Bobby Cox, Leo Durocher, Rube Foster, Tommy Lasorda, Connie Mack,
Billy Martin, Joe McCarthy, John McGraw, and Casey Stengel.
    ISBN 0-7660-1076-7
    1. Baseball managers—United States—Biography—Juvenile literature.
    2. Baseball managers—Rating of—United States—Juvenile literature.
    [1. Baseball managers] I. Title. II. Series.
GV865.A1P474   1999
796.357'092'273—dc21
[B]   98-3015
                                      CIP
                                        AC

To Our Readers:
All Internet addresses in this book were active and appropriate when we
went to press. Any comments or suggestions can be sent by e-mail to
Comments@enslow.com or to the address on the back cover.

The Publisher

Illustration Credits: AP/Wide World Photos, p. 9; Atlanta Braves, p. 13;
Collection of the author, pp. 39, 41; Courtesy Guy Barbieri, p. 25; J. Sebo/
Atlanta Braves, p. 10; Montreal Expos, p. 6; National Baseball Library
Cooperstown, N.Y./Oakland Athletics Archives, p. 29; Oakland Athletics
Archives, pp. 31, 33; Richard Collins, pp. 17, 23, 43, 45; TRANSCENDENTAL
GRAPHICS, pp. 15, 18, 21, 27, 35, 37.

Cover Illustration: Oakland Athletics Archives

Cover Description: Billy Martin, as manager of the Oakland Athletics

Interior Design: Richard Stalzer

CONTENTS

INTRODUCTION

MANAGING A MAJOR LEAGUE BASEBALL TEAM is one of the most difficult jobs in sports. Each manager must know the strengths and weaknesses of his own players and of every other player in the league. He must know when to hit and run, when to bunt, and when to take out a pitcher. He must deal with superstars who make millions of dollars a year and with reserve players who just want a chance to play. He must also deal with umpires, club owners, and newspaper and television reporters. And unlike other sports' coaches and managers, he must do it all in a grueling 162-game schedule.

Despite all this, just about every baseball fan (including even those with just the slightest knowledge of the game) feels free to second-guess these men. Second-guessing the manager is part of the fun of being a baseball fan.

Top 10 Baseball Managers takes a look at some of the national pastime's most skillful managers—from gentlemanly Connie Mack to combative, brawling Billy Martin, from colorful Tommy Lasorda to low-key Bobby Cox. There's no one correct way of managing—even in a particular era, or even by a particular manager. Circumstances are constantly changing. So are the personalities that a manager has to handle.

When the great Joe McCarthy managed the Yankees to pennant after pennant, he insisted that his players maintain a sense of Yankee pride—and dignity. All Yankees had to wear ties and suit jackets when they traveled on the road. In 1948, however, McCarthy moved over to manage the rival Boston Red Sox, where slugger Ted Williams was famous for refusing to wear neckties.

Everyone wanted to see what McCarthy would do. In spring training he came into the Red Sox dining room. Not only was McCarthy not wearing a tie—he was wearing the loudest sport coat he could find. "If I can't get along with a .400 hitter," said McCarthy, "it'll be my fault."[1]

Just about everything that goes wrong with a major-league ballclub is the manager's fault—or at least that's what his critics say. Not everyone would agree to choose these ten men for their top ten lists. But the ten we have chosen—like McCarthy and the other nine managers chronicled here—have also done an awful lot right.

CAREER STATISTICS

Manager	Seasons	Wins	Losses	PCT.	Pennants	World Series
FELIPE ALOU*	6	470	399	.541	0	0
BOBBY COX*	15	1,312	1,089	.546	4	1
LEO DUROCHER	24	2,009	1,709	.540	3	1
RUBE FOSTER†	–	–	–	–	–	–
TOMMY LASORDA	21	1,599	1,439	.526	4	3
CONNIE MACK	53	3,731	3,948	.486	9	5
BILLY MARTIN	16	1,253	1,013	.553	2	1
JOE MCCARTHY	24	2,125	1,333	.615	9	7
JOHN MCGRAW	33	2,763	1,948	.586	12	3
CASEY STENGEL	25	1,905	1,842	.508	10	7

*=Through 1997 Season
†=Negro League Manager, statistics unavailable

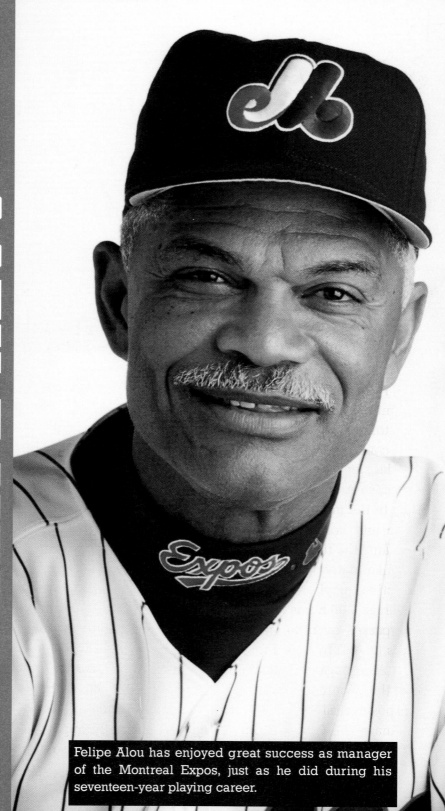

FELIPE ALOU

Felipe Alou has enjoyed great success as manager of the Montreal Expos, just as he did during his seventeen-year playing career.

BASEBALL IS A FAMILY AFFAIR to Expos manager Felipe Alou. His brothers—Matty and Jesus—also played in the major leagues (in fact, on September 10, 1963, all three brothers came to bat in the same inning for the San Francisco Giants). With the Expos, Alou has managed not only his own son, talented outfielder Moises Alou, but also his nephew, relief pitcher Mel Rojas. When he managed Moises, Felipe Alou became only the fifth father in Major League history to manage his son.

Felipe Alou grew up desperately poor in his native Dominican Republic in the Caribbean. He wanted to be a doctor, but when he starred in the Pan-American Games for his country, the New York Giants offered him a two hundred dollar signing bonus. The money meant a lot to someone so poor, so Alou signed with the Giants.

In the minors, the dark-skinned Alou faced discrimination and hostility in the American South. Eventually, he became the first Dominican to play regularly in the majors. Unlike many successful managers, he enjoyed a very productive playing career, posting a lifetime .286 batting average, 206 home runs, and 852 RBIs in 2,082 games. Until surpassed by Julio Franco, Alou held the record for most hits (2,101) by a Dominican native.

Alou began his coaching and managing career in 1979 in the Montreal organization, and he has been with the Expos ever since—even turning down a chance in 1985 to manage the Giants. In 1992, the Expos finally appointed him as their manager. Despite working for a franchise with young players and a very low player payroll (even Moises Alou and Mel Rojas had to leave Montreal to obtain higher salaries), Alou has helped to keep the Expos competitive. "Leadership to me is being able to get the job done," Alou said. "If we do that, it doesn't matter if our players are young or not."[1]

In 1994, the Associated Press, the BBWAA, and *The Sporting News*, named Alou the Major League Manager of the Year. In 1995, he managed the National League All-Star team to a 3–2 victory over the American League. Then, in 1998, Alou became the winningest manager in Expos history.

"Felipe is always one step ahead," said former Expos third baseman Tim Wallach, "He doesn't wait until the other team makes its move. He's the aggressor and he forces the other team's hand.[2]

FELIPE ALOU

BORN: May 12, 1935, Haina, Dominican Republic.

PLAYING CAREER: San Francisco Giants, 1958–1963;
    Milwaukee/Atlanta Braves, 1964–1969; Oakland A's,
    1970–1971; New York Yankees, 1971–1973; Montreal Expos,
    1973; Milwaukee Brewers, 1974.

TEAMS MANAGED: Montreal Expos, 1992– .

AWARDS AND ACHIEVEMENTS: Florida State League Manager of the
    Year, 1990. *The Sporting News* NL Manager of the Year,
    1994. BBWAA NL Manager of the Year, 1994.

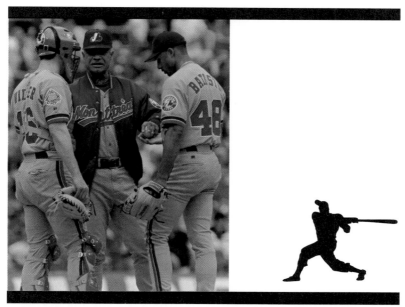

Felipe Alou talks over the strategy with catcher Chris Widger and
pitcher Miguel Batista. Alou is one of many in his family to be
involved in Major League Baseball.

Internet Site (for more information about Felipe Alou):
http://www.montrealexpos.com/playball/eqp/eqp97/bios/alou_f.htm

BOBBY COX

Prior to the success he has had with the team in the 1990s, Cox managed the Atlanta Braves in the late 1970s and early 1980s.

BOBBY COX

MANY OF THE MANAGERS IN THE 1990S are bigger "names" than Atlanta's Bobby Cox—Jim Leyland, Tony LaRussa, Joe Torre—but none can match the tremendous success Cox has enjoyed as Atlanta Braves manager. "Don't let that good-ol'-boy style fool you," says Atlanta Braves president Stan Kasten. "He is one sharp operator."[1]

In 1959, Cox received a forty thousand dollar bonus—then a huge amount—to sign with the Dodgers. He spent seven seasons in the Los Angeles system, then was traded to Atlanta. He did not reach the majors, however, until 1968, when he became the Yankees' third baseman. After his major-league playing career ended, he remained in the Yankees farm system as a player and a manager. He returned to the Yankees in 1977 to coach under Billy Martin. The following year, the Braves hired Cox to manage their club. He lasted four seasons but never finished higher than fourth before moving over to pilot the Toronto Blue Jays in the American League. In 1985, Cox's Jays captured the AL East title, the first time a non-United States team had won an MLB division championship. That season, the Associated Press named Cox as Major League Manager of the Year.

Surprisingly, Cox then quit as Blue Jays manager and became the Braves' general manager. In 1990, though, he returned to the dugout as Braves field manager. In 1991, Cox led the Braves to their first pennant since 1958—and began a run of six division championships in six straight completed seasons (the 1994 season was not completed because of that year's baseball strike). Cox's Braves surprised everyone by defeating the powerhouse Cleveland Indians in the 1995 World Series.

In 1996, the Braves again finished first in the NL East, and went on to win the National League pennant. The following year, 1997, Cox's Braves posted a 101–61 won-lost record, again finishing first in the NL East. After defeating Houston in the Division Series, the Braves lost to the surprising Florida Marlins, 4 games to 2, in the National League Championship Series (NLCS).

"If you can't play for Bobby, you've got a problem," Atlanta pitcher Tom Glavine once remarked. "He's every bit a players' manager. He's very simple in what he wants: show up on time, be ready to play, and give it 100 percent. If you do that, he's in your corner. He treats you like a man and expects you to respect what he wants. You just go out there and play hard."[2]

BOBBY COX

BORN: May 21, 1941, Tulsa, Oklahoma.

PLAYING CAREER: New York Yankees, 1968–1969.

TEAMS MANAGED: Atlanta Braves, 1978–1981, 1990– ; Toronto Blue Jays, 1982–1985.

AWARDS AND ACHIEVEMENTS: *The Sporting News* Major League Manager of the Year, 1985. BBWAA AL Manager of the Year, 1985. *The Sporting News* NL Manager of the Year, 1991, 1993. BBWAA NL Manager of the Year, 1991.

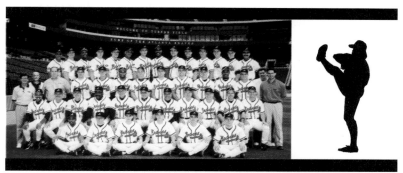

In the 1990s, Bobby Cox's teams have won one World Series, in 1995, and made the Fall Classic three other years.

Internet Site (for more information about Bobby Cox):
http://www.atlantabraves.com/web/lineup/players/cox.b.html

LEO DUROCHER

"NICE GUYS FINISH LAST," is what Leo "The Lip" Durocher once said in describing a fellow manager.[1] The same phrase has been used to sum up Durocher's philosophy on life.

Durocher would do anything to win ("Win any way you can, so long as you can get away with it."),[2] and off the field he was no angel either. Many of his friends were shady characters and gamblers. In 1947, Baseball Commissioner "Happy" Chandler got so fed up with Durocher he banned him from the game for the entire season.

Durocher was rough, but he could motivate a team to win. In 1941, he led the Brooklyn Dodgers to their first pennant in twenty-one years. Ten years later, Durocher (now the manager of Brooklyn's archrivals, the New York Giants) managed his club to an unlikely pennant as the Giants came from 13.5 games back to catch the Dodgers. In 1954, Durocher's Giants again won the National League pennant. In the World Series they were underdogs to the powerful Cleveland Indians (who won 111 regular-season games—an American League record). But Durocher's team won four straight to capture the world championship.

During his playing career Durocher was a good-field, no-hit shortstop. When he began his major-league career with the New York Yankees in 1925, Babe Ruth called him the "all-American out." Soon the Yankees waived Durocher to Cincinnati. In 1933, the cash-strapped Reds traded him to the St. Louis Cardinals. The slick-fielding Durocher helped the rough-and-tumble "Gas House Gang" Cards to a pennant in 1934.

Durocher joined the Brooklyn Dodgers in 1938. The

The hard-nosed Leo Durocher led both the Brooklyn Dodgers and their archrivals, the New York Giants, to National League pennants.

LEO DUROCHER

following year he became their player-manager—and the once-forlorn Dodgers became winners. Brooklyn won the 1941 pennant. The following year the team won 104 games—but finished only second.

In the spring of 1947, Durocher urged his players to accept modern baseball's first African American—Jackie Robinson—on the team. Robinson made the team—and history—but Durocher found himself suspended for the season because he refused to stop associating with gamblers. Shortly after Durocher returned to Brooklyn in 1948, he shocked Dodgers fans by leaving to manage the Giants. With New York, Durocher proved crucial to the success of Hall of Fame center fielder Willie Mays. Mays was very young and unsure of himself when he first reached the big leagues, but Durocher had faith in him and restored Mays's faith in himself.

Durocher left the Giants after the 1955 season and became a television sportscaster. Later he coached for the Los Angeles Dodgers (they had moved out of Brooklyn after the 1957 season). In 1966, The Lip returned to managing with the Chicago Cubs. In 1969, his Cubs seemed like a sure thing to win the NL pennant but instead finished behind Gil Hodges's Miracle Mets. Durocher finished his managerial career with the 1973 Houston Astros.

LEO DUROCHER

BORN: July 27, 1905, West Springfield, Massachusetts.

DIED: October 7, 1991, Palm Springs, California.

PLAYING CAREER: New York Yankees, 1925, 1928–1929; Cincinnati Reds, 1930–1933; St. Louis Cardinals, 1933–1937; Brooklyn Dodgers, 1938–1941, 1943, 1945.

TEAMS MANAGED: Brooklyn Dodgers, 1939–1946, 1948; New York Giants, 1948–1955; Chicago Cubs, 1966–1972; Houston Astros, 1972–1973.

AWARDS AND ACHIEVEMENTS: *The Sporting News* Major League Manager of the Year, 1939, 1954. Baseball Hall of Fame, elected 1994.

Leo Durocher urged his players to accept Jackie Robinson as a member of the Dodgers.

Internet Site (for more information about Leo Durocher):
http://www.cmgww.com/baseball/durocher/durocher.html

RUBE FOSTER

Rube Foster was influential in the formation of the Negro baseball leagues. In 1920, he founded the Negro National League (NNL) and became its first president.

ANDREW "RUBE" FOSTER NEVER MANAGED—or played—
an inning of Major League Baseball, but we still consider
him to be one of the game's top ten managers.

Foster was African American, and before 1947 African
Americans were not allowed to play in "organized baseball."
Instead, they formed their own teams and leagues and produced such great stars as Satchel Paige, Josh Gibson, and
Rube Foster. Foster is now usually remembered as a great
Negro Leagues manager and as the founder and president of
the Negro National League. He was also a highly talented
right-handed pitcher. In 1902, Foster won 44 straight games
for the Cuban Union Giants. In 1905, he posted a 51–5
record for the Philadelphia Giants.

Foster began his managing career in 1907 for a brand-
new club, the Leland Giants of Chicago. The team posted an
amazing 110–10 record. In 1910, the club was even better,
going 123–6. Foster renamed the team the Chicago American
Giants in 1911. This team captured championships in both
1914 and 1917 and shared the 1915 title with the New York
Lincoln Stars. To his team, Foster emphasized speed and
knowledge of baseball's fundamentals. "All his players,"
observed baseball historian James Riley, "were required to
master the bunt and the hit-and-run, and he expected
runners to go from first to third on the hit-and-run and the
bunt-and-run."[1]

Foster decided to organize an entire league, a league that
would feature both African-American players and managers—and African-American owners. On February 13,
1920, he founded the Negro National League and became its

first president. The NNL quickly became the most powerful league in African-American baseball. "We are the ship," the league's motto read, "all else the sea."[2]

Foster ruled the NNL with an iron hand. He was not only NNL president but also league secretary. At the same time he remained president, general manager, and field manager of the Chicago American Giants. His teams won pennants in 1921 and 1922 and the second-half championship in 1926. On the American Giants was Foster's half brother, southpaw Bill Foster, who in 1926 won 26 straight games. Bill Foster was elected to Baseball's Hall of Fame in 1996.

In 1926, Rube Foster grew ill and had to be hospitalized. He died in 1930, nearly seventeen years before Jackie Robinson finally integrated the major leagues.

In 1981, Rube Foster was elected to the National Baseball Hall of Fame.

RUBE FOSTER

BORN: September 17, 1879, Calvert, Texas.

DIED: December 9, 1930, Kankakee, Illinois.

PLAYING CAREER: Cuban Union Giants, Cuban X-Giants,
Philadelphia Giants, Chicago Leland Giants.

TEAMS MANAGED: Chicago Leland Giants, Chicago American
Giants.

AWARDS AND ACHIEVEMENTS: Baseball Hall of Fame, elected 1981.

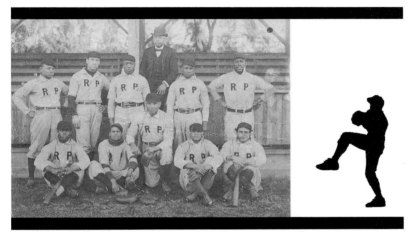

Rube Foster (back row, third from left) was not only a manager and leader of the Negro Leagues, but also a dominant pitcher. In 1905, he won 51 games for the Philadelphia Giants, an amazing number of victories.

Internet Site (for more information about Rube Foster):
http://www.majorleaguebaseball.com/nbl/nl11.sml

TOMMY LASORDA

ON THE WAY TO BECOMING baseball's goodwill ambassador, the Dodgers' Tommy Lasorda proved to be a pretty good manager—winning six division championships, four pennants, and two World Series.

Lasorda's major-league pitching career was very brief, but his minor-league career was long and often distinguished. In 1948, with the Schenectady Blue Jays, Lasorda struck out 25 batters in 15 innings. With stuff like that, you may wonder why he never starred in the majors. But Lasorda was wild. In that same game he walked 12 batters. Poor control plagued him for his entire career.

Nonetheless, Lasorda loved baseball, and he kept at it when many other players would have moved on to another line of work. The Los Angeles Dodgers rewarded Lasorda's perseverance by making him a manager in their farm system and later a coach with the big club. In the minors, Lasorda helped develop such future Dodgers stars as first baseman Steve Garvey, second baseman Davey Lopes, third baseman Ron Cey, and shortstop Bill Russell. When veteran Los Angeles manager Walter Alston retired in September 1976, Lasorda became the Dodgers' manager. Like Alston, Lasorda only worked on one-year contracts. His critics believed Lasorda would not be around long because he was too friendly with his players. Lasorda disagreed. "I don't believe there's a law that says a manager can't be friendly with his players and still command their respect."[1]

Lasorda predicted he would win the pennant in his first full season as Dodgers manager. He was right, but his Dodgers fell to the Yankees in six games in that fall's World

Tommy Lasorda managed the Dodgers for twenty years, retiring in 1996 for health reasons.

TOMMY LASORDA

Series. He later led his team to more division titles: in 1978, 1981, 1983, 1985, 1988, and 1995; National League pennants in 1978, 1981, and 1988; and World Series championships in 1981 and 1988.

His 1988 season may have been the most dramatic. In the League Championship Series, Lasorda's underdog Dodgers upset the favored New York Mets. Then, in the ninth inning of the first game of the World Series against the Oakland A's, Lasorda sent up badly injured Kirk Gibson to pinch hit. Gibson homered to win the game, and he gave the Dodgers the momentum to win the entire Fall Classic.

Lasorda retired in the middle of the 1996 season after suffering a heart attack. He was elected to the Baseball Hall of Fame in 1997. In 1998, he was hired as the Dodgers general manager.

"I bleed Dodger blue," Lasorda often said, "and when I die, I'm going to the Big Dodger in the sky."[2]

TOMMY LASORDA

BORN: September 22, 1927, Norristown, Pennsylvania.

PLAYING CAREER: Brooklyn Dodgers, 1954–1955; Kansas City A's, 1956.

TEAMS MANAGED: Los Angeles Dodgers, 1976–1996.

AWARDS AND ACHIEVEMENTS: *The Sporting News* Minor League Manager of the Year, 1970. BBWAA NL Manager of the Year, 1983, 1988. *The Sporting News* NL Co-Manager of the Year, 1988. Baseball Hall of Fame, elected 1997.

Before Tommy Lasorda's days of managing the Dodgers, he pitched in the minors and majors. Lasorda is in front, at the left.

Internet Site (for more information about Tommy Lasorda): http://www.baseballhalloffame.org/members/hofers/tcl/tcl.html

CONNIE MACK

IF YOU WERE TO PICTURE the average baseball manager, you would not picture Connie Mack. After his last year as a player-manager in 1896, Cornelius Alexander McGillicuddy (Connie Mack's real name) never again wore a baseball uniform to manage. He dressed in an ordinary suit with a high starched collar. He never went onto the field to change a pitcher or argue with an umpire (he couldn't, because he was not in uniform). He held onto his job with the Philadelphia Athletics (A's) for a record fifty seasons and ended up owning the team. He never swore and rarely raised his voice at his players. To position his fielders, he did not use a computer (they had not yet been invented)— he just used his phenomenal baseball memory and moved fielders into position by gently waving a scorecard in one direction or another.

Connie Mack had started out as a good-field, no-hit catcher in the 1880s. Even then he was strategizing—and not always in the most honest fashion. Sometimes he would freeze baseballs before throwing them into play for opposing batters to hit. The cold deadened the balls and made them harder to hit with authority.

Mack managed the Pittsburgh Pirates in the 1890s and the Milwaukee Brewers in 1900, but he is best known for managing the old Philadelphia Athletics from 1901 to 1950. With Mack and his A's, life seemed to be all-or-nothing. They won nine pennants—but also finished last seventeen times.

Mack created his first dynasty when Philadelphia captured pennants in 1910, 1911, 1913, and 1914. He won the

CONNIE MACK

Unlike other managers, Connie Mack never dressed in a uniform. He preferred to wear a suit in the dugout, and always stood out alongside his players.

World Series in 1910, 1911, and 1913, twice defeating John McGraw's Giants. Yet after losing the 1914 Series to the underdog Boston Braves, Mack broke up his team. "I was sore," Mack later admitted. "I wanted a winner."[1]

The team fell into the basement. But in 1929, with a new cast of players, Mack once again led the A's to the pennant. His most famous strategizing came during that year's World Series against Joe McCarthy's Chicago Cubs. Everybody expected Mack to start his ace pitcher, Lefty Grove, in Game 1. Mack shocked everyone by starting washed-up right-handed sidearm pitcher Howard Ehmke. To Mack, the move made perfect sense. He knew that Chicago had a lineup of only right-handed hitters. Righties often have trouble hitting pitchers who employ a sidearm delivery. Ehmke came through, winning the game, 3–1, and striking out a then-record 14 batters. It was the thirty-five-year-old Ehmke's last big-league win. After the Series, Mack won the prestigious Edward W. Bok Award as the individual who had performed the greatest service for the city of Philadelphia.

Connie Mack won pennants again in 1930 and 1931, but he broke up his team once again. The Depression reduced attendance for A's games, and Mack sold off his great stars— Lefty Grove, slugger Jimmie Foxx, catcher Mickey Cochrane, and outfielder Al Simmons. Mack's A's never won another pennant.

"He never mixed with his players," recalled pitcher Bob Shawkey, "but at the same time he always had tremendous morale on his clubs. He knew how to handle men. He was very shrewd, and gentle, and always talked to you like a father. The boys worshipped him."[2]

The eighty-five-year-old Mack, who had been elected to the Hall of Fame in 1937, retired after the 1950 season. He died in 1956.

CONNIE MACK

BORN: December 22, 1862, East Brookfield, Massachusetts.

DIED: February 8, 1956, Germantown, Pennsylvania.

PLAYING CAREER: Washington Senators, 1886–1889; Buffalo Bisons, 1890; Pittsburgh Pirates, 1891–1896.

TEAMS MANAGED: Pittsburgh Pirates, 1894–1896; Milwaukee Brewers, 1900; Philadelphia A's, 1901–1950.

AWARDS AND ACHIEVEMENTS: Edward W. Bok Award in 1929. Baseball Hall of Fame, elected 1937.

Connie Mack managed the Philadelphia A's with quiet dignity for fifty years. While other managers would argue calls made by the umpires or yell at their players, Mack always maintained his composure.

Internet Site (for more information about Connie Mack):
http://www.majorleaguebaseball.com/digest/mack.sml

BILLY MARTIN

BILLY MARTIN WAS THE BAD BOY of Baseball. He produced winning teams wherever he managed, but alienated both players and owners with his fiery personality. "Some people have a chip on their shoulder," wrote columnist Jim Murray. "Billy has a lumberyard."[1]

Martin began his playing career in the 1950s as a versatile infielder with Casey Stengel's championship Yankees teams. Yet after Martin was involved in a famous brawl at New York's Copacabana nightclub in 1957, the Yankees exiled him to the second-division Kansas City A's. Even after that he always considered himself to be a Yankee.

His first big-league managerial job was with the Minnesota Twins. In his first year, he took his team from seventh place to first. Still, he was fired. He made winners out of the Tigers and the Rangers. Again ownership fired him.

In 1975, Yankees owner George Steinbrenner hired Martin to manage the Bronx Bombers. Martin was thrilled to be back with his old club. In 1976, his first full season with New York, he led the Yankees to their first pennant since 1964.

The Yankees won the world championship in 1977, but controversy still dogged Martin. He battled with Steinbrenner, and he battled with his slugging superstar, Reggie Jackson. Once, on live national television, Martin and the much-larger Jackson nearly came to blows inside the Yankees dugout.

Steinbrenner ended up hiring—and firing—Martin six times between 1975 and 1988. The situation became a nationwide joke.

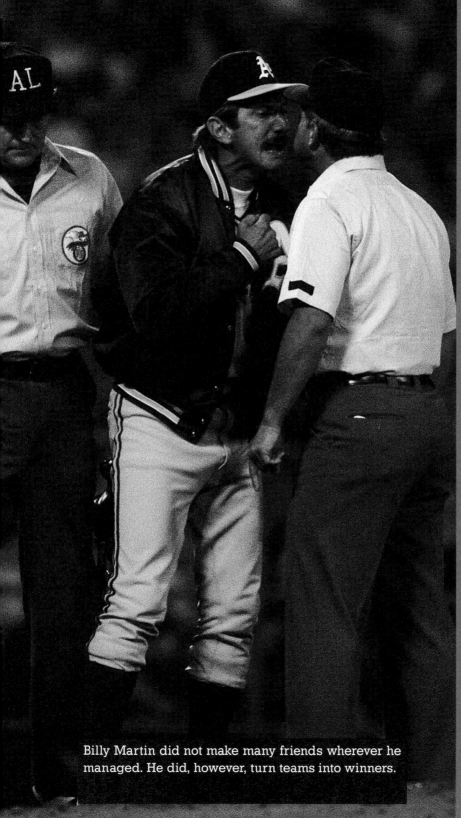

BILLY MARTIN

Billy Martin did not make many friends wherever he managed. He did, however, turn teams into winners.

In 1980, Martin became manager of the Oakland A's. Once again he turned a losing team into a winner, using a hustling strategy known as Billy Ball. The A's became the 1981 AL West champs. Even then he was fired a year later—as critics charged he had burned out his starting pitchers by leaving them in too long. Whatever controversy followed him, Billy "the Kid" Martin refused to change his combative ways. "I can't change now," he once said. "I guess it's like being a gunfighter. Once you start, you do it for life—until somebody comes along and shoots you down."[2]

Martin died on Christmas Day, 1989, in a car crash near his home in upstate New York.

"Billy was a true Yankee—one of the truest ever," said shortstop Bucky Dent. "He always said he wanted to die a Yankee. He was his own man. He was fiery and could be charming. He was a great manager."[3]

BILLY MARTIN

BORN: May 16, 1928, Berkeley, California.

DIED: December 25, 1989, Johnson City, New York.

PLAYING CAREER: New York Yankees, 1950–1953, 1955–1957; Kansas
City A's, 1957; Detroit Tigers, 1958; Cleveland Indians, 1959;
Cincinnati Reds, 1960; Milwaukee Braves, 1961; Minnesota
Twins, 1961.

TEAMS MANAGED: Minnesota Twins, 1969; Detroit Tigers,
1971–1973; Texas Rangers, 1973–1975; New York Yankees,
1975–1979, 1983, 1985, 1988; Oakland A's, 1980–1982.

AWARDS AND ACHIEVEMENTS: *The Sporting News* Major League
Manager of the Year, 1981.

Billy Martin managed five teams during his lifetime. He is most
remembered for managing the Oakland Athletics and the New
York Yankees.

Internet Site (for more information about Billy Martin):
http://www.cmgww.com/baseball/martin/martin.html

JOE MCCARTHY

OF ALL THE MANAGERS in *Top 10 Baseball Managers*, only Joe McCarthy and Rube Foster never played even a single game in the major leagues. "Wasn't good enough, I guess," he once said, "but I spent more time trying to get up there than almost anyone I can think of."[1] When he first began to manage in the big leagues, rival managers and players called him a "bush leaguer," suggesting that he didn't belong in the majors. He soon proved them wrong.

Very wrong. Joe McCarthy stills holds the record for most world championship teams managed, with seven (a record he shares with Casey Stengel); the record for the all-time best regular-season career won-lost percentage (.615); and the record for the best career World Series won-lost percentage (.698). He was even the first manager to win pennants in both the National and American Leagues.

McCarthy began managing in the minors in 1919. In 1926, he was hired to manage the Chicago Cubs. Three years later, this "bush leaguer" had led the Cubs to their first pennant since 1918.

In 1931, McCarthy became manager of the New York Yankees, who—despite the presence of Babe Ruth and slugging first baseman Lou Gehrig on the team—had not won a pennant since 1928. The following year McCarthy led them to a world championship—and a sweep of his old club, the Cubs, in the World Series. But McCarthy did not really get started until four years later. From 1936 through 1943, McCarthy's Yankees captured seven American League pennants and six world championships. His jealous critics no longer called McCarthy a "busher." Now they called him a

JOE McCARTHY

Joe McCarthy led one of the most talented teams in baseball, the New York Yankees of the 1930s and 1940s. Under McCarthy, the team won six World Series titles.

"push-button manager." By that they meant that he only won because he had very talented players, such as Lou Gehrig, center fielder Joe DiMaggio, and pitcher Lefty Gomez.

But McCarthy had great managerial skills. He instilled great pride in his players, maintained discipline without being too harsh, and was a master at handling players. "I loved him," former Yankees outfielder Tommy Henrich once recalled. "One of the greatest men I ever knew. I don't know where in the heck he learned all his psychology about ballplayers. He could handle almost anybody. And if he couldn't handle them he'd trade them."[2]

McCarthy left the Yankees during the 1946 season but came out of retirement to manage the Boston Red Sox. He missed pennants by a single game in both 1948 and 1949. Elected to the Hall of Fame in 1957, he died in 1978.

Joe McCarthy

Born: April 21, 1887, Philadelphia, Pennsylvania.

Died: January 13, 1978, Buffalo, New York.

Teams Managed: Chicago Cubs, 1926–1930; New York Yankees, 1931–1946; Boston Red Sox, 1948–1950.

Awards and Achievements: *The Sporting News* Major League Manager of the Year, 1936, 1938, 1943. Baseball Hall of Fame, elected 1957.

Although he never played a single game in the major leagues, Joe McCarthy achieved great success as a manager, especially with the New York Yankees.

Internet Site (for more information about Joe McCarthy): http://www.baseballhalloffame.org/members/hofers/jvm/jvm.html

JOHN MCGRAW

JOHN MCGRAW ENJOYED BEING CALLED the Little Napoleon of Baseball, outthinking opposing managers and players. His feisty leadership style made his New York Giants into an early baseball dynasty and made him into the most feared manager in the major leagues.

Before becoming a Hall of Fame manager, John "Muggsy" McGraw started as a rough-and-tumble third baseman on the legendary Baltimore Orioles of the 1890s. The Orioles played rough—and they played to win. To reach base McGraw would do anything—bunt, foul off pitch after pitch (to eventually draw a walk), or purposely get hit by a pitch. When enemy base runners would round third, McGraw would even grab their belts to slow them down.

When the American League became a major league in 1901, its Baltimore franchise hired McGraw as its manager. But league president Ban Johnson frowned on the way the Little Napoleon battled with AL umpires. Soon McGraw was back in the National League, as manager of the New York Giants.

Before McGraw's arrival, the Giants had been a losing team. McGraw transformed the franchise into a winner. He helped develop right-hander Christy Mathewson into a standout pitcher, and he later discovered such stars as second baseman Frankie Frisch, first baseman Bill Terry, and right fielder Ross Youngs—all Hall of Famers.

McGraw prided himself on his strategizing, his use of the hit-and-run, the bunt, the stolen base, the pickoff, and so on. These were all popular when he himself had been

JOHN McGRAW

John McGraw was player/manager of the New York Giants from 1902–06, before becoming strictly the team's field general.

playing in the 1890s. When Babe Ruth—and the long ball—revolutionized baseball strategy in the 1920s, McGraw refused to adapt to changing times. He had contempt for Ruth and his prodigious homers, preferring to stick with the kind of baseball he knew best—"inside baseball," he called it.

McGraw could be a tough opponent, but he could also be a good friend. He would not tolerate mental errors, but he never held a physical error against a player. He would also aid numerous down-on-their-luck former ballplayers with generous "loans"—loans that were often never repaid.

"He helped everyone," recalled slugging Giants outfielder Mel Ott, "even those he disliked. He was a fine, decent man and the greatest thing that ever happened to me was knowing him. He was the greatest manager baseball has ever known. Nobody could inspire players the way he could and give them such a will to win."[1]

McGraw, in poor health, retired during the 1932 season. He died in 1934 and was elected to the Hall of Fame in 1937.

JOHN McGRAW

BORN: April 7, 1873, Truxton, New York.

DIED: February 25, 1934, New Rochelle, New York.

PLAYING CAREER: Baltimore Orioles (American Association), 1891; Baltimore Orioles (National League), 1892–1899; St. Louis Cardinals, 1900; Baltimore Orioles (American League), 1901–1902; New York Giants, 1902–1906.

TEAMS MANAGED: Baltimore Orioles (National League), 1899; Baltimore Orioles (American League), 1901–1902; New York Giants, 1902–1932.

AWARDS AND ACHIEVEMENTS: Baseball Hall of Fame, elected 1937.

McGraw (left) talks over strategy with fellow Hall of Fame member Honus Wagner. McGraw led the Giants to three World Series victories.

Internet Site (for more information about John McGraw):
http://www.baseballhalloffame.org/members/hofers/jjm2/jjm2.html

CASEY STENGEL

SOME PEOPLE THOUGHT CASEY STENGEL was a clown. That all changed when he took over the New York Yankees in 1949 and led them to a record five straight world championships. Then they thought he was a genius.

Actually, Stengel *had* been a clown. When he played the outfield in the majors from 1912–1925, he pulled such stunts as hiding a sparrow in his cap. When the crowd booed him, he took off his cap, and the bird flew out. The boos turned to cheers.

But Stengel was also a very good player. He hit two homers in the 1923 World Series—including one inside-the-park job. He was a smart ballplayer, one who soaked up every bit of baseball knowledge he could from such managers as Brooklyn's Wilbert Robinson and New York's legendary John McGraw.

In the 1930s Stengel managed the Brooklyn Dodgers and then the Boston Braves, who were known as the Boston Bees for much of his career there. Both were bad teams, and Stengel's reputation worsened. He was now not only a clown—he was a loser. Stengel returned to the minors. Although he led Oakland to a Pacific Coast League pennant, it seemed he would never manage in the big leagues again.

Then Stengel got a call from an old friend, George Weiss. Weiss, now general manager of the Yankees, wanted Stengel to take over the club. Most sportswriters thought Weiss had lost his mind. Stengel was a joke who would run the once proud and dignified Yankees into the ground.

But Stengel proved his critics wrong. He perfected a system of managing called the platoon system. Instead of

Casey Stengel spent most of his managerial career in New York. He managed the Yankees, Mets, and Brooklyn Dodgers.

just putting eight position players out on the field day in and day out, Stengel would use his players only in certain situations—to get the best out of what were often limited talents. He would use right-handed hitters against left-handed pitchers (and vice versa). He would move players from one position to another—even such great players as Hall of Fame catcher Yogi Berra, whom Stengel often played in left field.

Stengel's system worked to perfection. From 1949–53 the Yankees won a record five straight world championships. Then they captured pennants every year from 1955–58 (and world championships in 1956 and 1958) and another American League championship in 1960.

After the club lost the 1960 World Series to Pittsburgh, the Yankees' management fired both Weiss and the seventy-year-old Stengel. "Most people my age are dead at the present time, and you could look it up,"[1] Casey joked, but he wasn't happy about losing his job.

He came out of retirement in 1962 and moved across town to manage the expansion New York Mets. It was not an easy job. This new franchise was terrible, losing a record 120 games in their first season. "Can't anybody play this here game?"[2] Stengel wailed.

The Mets continued to lose, but still Stengel was a real asset to the franchise. He used his wit and charm to shift attention away from just how bad his team was. He retired in 1965 after breaking his hip in a fall and was elected to the Hall of Fame in 1966.

BORN: July 30, 1890, Kansas City, Missouri.

DIED: September 29, 1975, Glendale, California.

PLAYING CAREER: Brooklyn Dodgers, 1912–1917; Pittsburgh Pirates, 1918–1919; Philadelphia Phillies, 1920–1921; New York Giants, 1921–1923; Boston Braves, 1924–1925.

TEAMS MANAGED: Brooklyn Dodgers, 1934–1936; Boston Braves (Bees), 1938–1943; New York Yankees, 1949–1960; New York Mets, 1962–1965.

AWARDS AND ACHIEVEMENTS: *The Sporting News* Major League Manager of the Year, 1949, 1953, 1958. Baseball Hall of Fame, elected 1966.

Casey Stengel was loved by the city of New York, and he was as well known for his antics as he was for his success.

Internet Site (for more information about Casey Stengel): http://www.cmgww.com/baseball/stengel/stengel.html

CHAPTER NOTES

Introduction

1. Ted Williams (as told to John Underwood), *My Turn at Bat: The Story of My Life* (New York: Simon & Schuster, 1988), p. 130.

Felipe Alou

1. Chuck Johnson, "Young Expos Find Guide in Alou," *USA Today*, March 1, 1993, p. 4C.

2. Chuck Johnson, "Young and the Restless; Expos Doing About-Face Under Alou," *USA Today*, August 7, 1992, p. 1C.

Bobby Cox

1. Rod Beaton, "Cox Voted NL's Top Manager," *USA Today*, October 30, 1991, p. 3C.

2. John Thorn, Pete Palmer, Michael Gershman, David Pietrusza, and Dan Schlossberg, *Total Braves* (New York: Penguin Books, 1996), p. 7.

Leo Durocher

1. Hank Nuwar, *Strategies of the Great Baseball Managers* (New York: Franklin Watts, 1988), pp. 102–103.

2. Bill Adler, *Baseball Wit* (New York: Crown, 1986), p. 118.

Rube Foster

1. James A. Riley, *The Biographical Encyclopedia of the Negro Baseball Leagues* (New York: Carroll & Graf, 1994), p. 291.

2. Robert Peterson, *Only the Ball Was White* (New York: Prentice-Hall, 1970), p. 83.

Tommy Lasorda

1. Tommy Lasorda and David Fisher, *The Artful Dodger* (New York: Arbor House, 1985), p. 189.

2. Paul Dickson, ed., *Baseball's Greatest Quotations* (New York: HarperCollins, 1991), p. 240.

Connie Mack

1. Charles B. Cleveland, *The Great Baseball Managers* (New York: Thomas Y. Crowell, 1950), p. 45.

2. Hank Nuwer, *Strategies of the Great Baseball Managers* (New York: Franklin Watts, 1988), pp. 30–31.

Billy Martin

1. Kevin Nelson, *Baseball's Greatest Insults* (New York: Simon & Schuster, 1984), p. 44.

2. Norman Lewis Smith, *The Return of Billy the Kid* (New York: Coward, McCann & Geoghegan, 1977), p. 213.

3. Paul Dickson, ed., *Baseball's Greatest Quotations* (New York: HarperCollins, 1991), p. 110.

Joe McCarthy

1. Donald Honig, *The Man in the Dugout* (Chicago: Follett, 1977), p. 81.

2. Donald Honig, *Baseball Between the Lines* (New York: Coward, McCann & Geoghegan, 1976), p. 29.

John McGraw

1. Harvey Frommer, *Baseball's Greatest Managers* (New York: Franklin Watts, 1985), p. 172.

Casey Stengel

1. Ira Berkow and Jim Kaplan, *The Gospel According to Casey* (New York: St. Martin's Press, 1992), p. 13.

2. Robert W. Creamer, *Stengel: His Life and Times* (New York: Simon & Schuster, 1984), p. 299.

INDEX